NIGHT FLOWERS

SOME FLOWERS, LIKE SOME PEOPLE,
SIMPLY BLOOM BETTER AT NIGHT.

----DEDICATION----

NIGHT FLOWERS IS PRESENTED AS A COUNTER TO
ALL THOSE THINGS THAT GO BUMP IN THE NIGHT.

THERE ARE SOME FLOWERS WHO SIMPLY BLOOM
BETTER AT NIGHT, JUST AS THERE ARE SOME
PEOPLE WHO SIMPLY BLOOM BETTER AT NIGHT.

DARKNESS DOES NOT ALWAYS REPRESENT EVIL
AND OFTEN DEMONSTRATES GREAT BEAUTY, AS
DO THESE NIGHT FLOWERS.

NIGHT FLOWERS MOSTLY LIVE THEIR LIVES IN
BEAUTY AND PASS WITHOUT NOTICE, JUST AS DO
MANY PEOPLE.

IT IS TO THOSE UNSEEN MILLIONS THAT THIS
WRITING IS DEDICATED.

ISBN-10: 1499302479
ISBN-13: 978-1499302479

CHAMPAGNE IRIS: PAINTING

CHAMPAGNE IRIS. PHOTO

SUNDOWN: THE PLACE WHERE OUR STORY BEGINS.

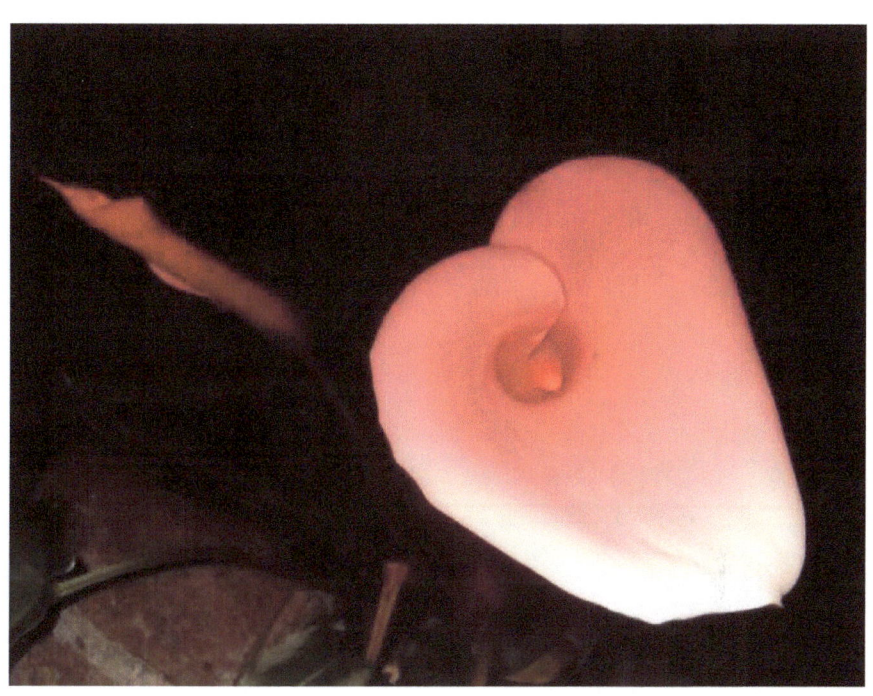

SUNRISE: THE PLACE WHERE OUR ONE NIGHT
JOURNEY ENDS.
GOOD DAY.

www.ingramcontent.com/pod-product-compliance
Lightning Source LLC
Chambersburg PA
CBHW051128290526
45796CB00001B/3